Natural
Beauty

Natural
Beauty

Conella Lyons

ARPress
45 Dan Road Suite 5
Canton MA 02021

Hotline: 1(888) 821-0229
Fax: 1(508) 545-7580

Ordering Information:
Quantity sales. Special discounts are available on quantity purchases by corporations, associations, and others. For details, contact the publisher at the address above.

Printed in the United States of America.
ISBN-13: Paperback 979-8-89330-791-7
          eBook   979-8-89330-792-4

Library of Congress Control Number: 2024904196

CONTENTS

Natural Beauty

T he Ant colony preparing to move pieces of the earth. This plan has been going on since the beginning of time. The Ant colony has selected a team leader to be head of these groups running various projects. This random selection has been developed over centuries to bring best results.

The Ant colony has begun preparation for removing pieces of broken up earth material. This selection involves movement of minute Earth particles been going on as a part of Ant culture since the beginning of time. The Ant population need a team leader to organize proper schedule of various production development engineering projects. The transporting pieces of material for movement to designated location zones for building. This construction project has been created by the ruling Ant hierarchy searching for best living environments. This project group planners organizing demolition phases of the project have spent several months searching areas for specific soil requirements. This special soil requirement will provide protection against elements of the earth atmosphere. The present existing environment has been determined too old for natures unpredictable climatic weather conditions. These abnormal weather conditions produced by natures abundant of rainy seasons create alternative living quarters for the supreme ruling hierarchy. This specific chosen choice of special earth selected for protection of new housing facilities has been analyzed to meet various qualifications required to ensure practical safety procedure. This soil has been undergoing rigorous test to maximize effectiveness needed by engineering team of ants assigned to remedy this situation for future housing occupation.

The game plan set up in blueprint by engineers should be followed strictly for best safety procedure. These engineers have been chosen for this project because of their levels of expertise in material hazard prevention standard requirement of quality control. The months involved in researching various parts of the regions to determine what soil would pass all qualifications of testing necessary to meet requirements needed for protection of ruling class housing location. This Ant team activists are committed to excellence which now determine their preparation in beginning of groundbreaking project in the new structural construction assignment.

The construction site has been under observation by various engineers and team leader's groups to determine best detonators available to destroy specific pieces of Earth. This demolition company has been manufacturing quality detonators for exceptional quality control requirements to excavate certain types of soil. The specific type of detonator selected upon to create most intense blasting for soil movement in preparation for underground living quarters. These experts will be coordinating experiences from previous demolition projects in hopes of continuing to mastermind best creative facilities ever known to Ant History. This innovative technique chosen to feature explosive has begun a futuristic approach for inventive wave of excellence. The development phase featuring construction in factories that manufacture detonators. This innovative expansive growth project created through Ant hierarchy should become so exponential of a boom in economic development for workers in Ant communities reaching throughout vast regions. The families gaining major economic prosperity will be living in best financial growth period over many years to come. This tremendous economic boom improving industrial development in so many future projects will further encourage Ant community into continuing recruitment for all phases of education.

The past economic slowdown has been unbelievably bad in helping to maintain stable economic family living conditions. This unstable economic lifestyle has affected young Ants creating horrible levels of criminal activities throughout Ant hierarchy dominion of power manipulation. This technology being invested into advancing economy for reducing criminal activities in this population. The engineers have been developing state of the arts manufacturing systems. This innovative production technology require education being established more in younger Ant society. The Ants gaining positions to operate latest technologically innovative system must understand standards required for best performance. This advanced system will allow opportunity for machines to be more productive in areas that normally required ants. This innovative technological breakthrough would create robots for faster productive standards that increase volume of manufacturing. This for see able futuristic technological innovation already in use in so many production-oriented atmosphere for increased volume in logistic for manufacturing process. The robotic culture will be so innovative structurally in manufacturing system for increasing production level far greater than older technology operations. The logistic development has created greater engineering prospects to maintain highest standard in manufacturing industry.

This Ant community recognition of unfair wealth division has created lack of opportunity through educational fields. The educational division represent wide scale diversity imposing insignificant progress in STEM (Science Technology English and Math) achievement movement due to bad economic leadership. This Science, Technology, English, and Math influence created lack of skilled laborers for special work projects. The failure on behalf of Ant Hierarchy to recognize imminent need for placing greater emphasis on education rather than correctional facilities. This business split in educational deprivation has been revealed throughout Ant hierarchy dominion for generations. This current shift in direction to respond with social media activist demonstration in persuading new agenda for accomplishing much better standard of living conditions. Ant activist seeking to bring family life standard up to equality with other community development progress will be reaping reward through benefits in health programs throughout social media interaction. This popular social media interaction became active source for critical response of bad community leadership. This influential social media reflexing on how wrong hierarchy excessive budget cutting affected community progression. The bad influence of overcrowded prison conditions made inner city family life so devastated from gang activities because of high dropout rates in many high school systems. The community leaders participating in campaigning on social media to escalate attention of Ant hierarchy appeal in regrouping form best ways to reconstruct living conditions. This process has been addressed to realize lack of economic stability necessary to accommodate genuine struggle because of division in relations. This crisis confronting Ant population in concern with equally sharing best possible need to boost up educational industry and community development fighting against criminal activities. The Ant hierarchy feeling crunch associated through this boom dealing with more major opportunity generating higher substantial employment from concentration on technologically innovative business projects. The skilled laborers needed to affectively respond to new state of the art equipment currently facing tremendous shortages for filling open positions. This economic opportunity has been responsible for increasing progress that would make employment development a major fulfillment to lower unskilled labor market.

These social issues have been constantly avoided because of lack of communication developing better results throughout decades. This involvement to create serious results by generating better candidates to campaign for office often time get swept underneath piles of other concerns and agendas. When elected officials get rewarded for running popular campaign slogan that never be fulfilled upon taking office. This bureaucracy has been effectively popular in reduction of economic prosperity by new officials that choose greediness instead of more popular campaign slogan which determined constituents electing these politicians to office. These politicians organize money making agendas that always destroy better economic opportunities for lower class citizens improving their community schools and other important living environment.

The Ant community leaders have found extremely impossible cooperation available through lack of attention being focused on lower income community agenda upon being elected by always representing minority of constituent population. This conspiracy approves complete domination of poor society citizens to avoid issue facing community crime recidivism continuing extremely high ratio in lower class area as opposed to better constituent neighborhood. The representation involves mostly majority of leaders failure in cooperating to realize less fortunate members cannot control enough popular authority required for necessary advantage point to become more powerful in recognizing an equal level for greater impact on changing neighborhood community.

The criminal justice system has been allowing poorer neighborhood constituents to continue being faced with overcrowded prisons because of seriously limited opportunity available in ghetto communities. This opportunity to become completely committed for organizing better economic resources to enhance equality requires more influential education standards available in high school that prepare students with the ability to be more competitive. This opportunity focusing on greater emphasis in achievement would further enhance student status that elevate practical understanding recognizing staying in school determine better chance to establish accomplishment of their dream in life. The Ant community challenge to prevent continuing deterioration of economy and infrastructure would lead to greater emphasis on recovery for generating higher degree level of family stability with environment creating upward mobility in household income category that make middle class status attainable. This improvement opportunity allowing family members income provision to be established with excellent sufficient financial gains for teenagers as well as adults to recognize fruitful benefits being created for better economic development of new hope accomplishment in family living environment.

The financial increase would allow teenagers a better advantage in focusing on career development opportunity available through STEM (Science, Technology, English, Math) resources provided with government assistance. This government assistance would be responsible when reliable candidates elected to office continuing to maintain standards that their agendas previously recommended to constituents. The Ant community constituents now can prepare equally for opportunity to be expressed by prioritization when accessing social media resources that actively share candidates campaign agendas to organize proper decision during debate for good or inaccurate information.

The opportunity developed by social media creation supplying current information through so many activities help increase volume of options available to share background check on reliable or unreliable government officials. This gratification sharing social media offer instant or prolonged destructive input into publicly elected officer career that allow probability to change history become so mind boggling.

These selfish egotistical government officials lack consideration to help our poorer class citizens improve their successful climb to gain equal opportunity that eventually develop great economic stability while generating reward upon completion of college education. This process to allow necessary beneficiary reward after graduation from college by allowing the American dream to be fulfilled with gainful employment when breaking into our economic workforce so education loans would be easily paid off.

These lower paying employment opportunity resort to inadequate payment of student loans that now need financially stable income for best ability necessary for maintaining sufficient payment plan of accountability after college graduation. This monetary crisis should be addressed more equally with greater emphasis placed on big businesses providing quality opportunity by supporting our country needs to progress with their billions of dollars escaping through tax loopholes. This cruel exploitation used to increase economic burden on poorer tax paying citizens result into reduction of necessary production opportunity required for bolstering our economy. The economic depletion initiated through good old boy successful accomplishment for greed association with business as usual to incorporate extraordinary lifestyle instead of facilitating greater emphasis on recovery of finances that strengthen our infrastructure. This incredible reluctance associated with allowing deterioration of our infrastructure results in increased shortage of professional construction contracts that need to be focused on expeditiously with attaining more skilled labor jobs. This American billionaire club organized to continue transfer of wealth status maintaining their emphasis always to allow big business to be able to continuously reward executives with overwhelming increases for extraordinary beneficial exploitation need to be suppressed immediately. These executive official primary minds of so many exclusive business opportunity schemes to further enhance their innovative manipulation in gratification procedure that maintain wealthy domination only within their social atmosphere. This financially robust manipulation incorporated through investment by the wealthy in United States of America shared by so few of the population. This will make taxes continue to be felt increasing and deliberately because of tax laws being passed to make sure this noose of a burden primarily handled by our hard working and struggling citizens. This wealthy percentage of financial burden crunching struggling citizens continue to be effectively functional because of the failure to vote which would determine destruction of a chaotic political policy that enforce so many free loopholes for wealthy constituents. This manipulative greed has been successfully incorporated for generations especially through financially accrued benefits from free slave labor providing extravagant family wealth status that flourished throughout the United States of America.

Summer Melt Down

The summertime life was about being free without any adults around to see kids doing the wrong thing. This was considered freedom for youngsters out of school over the summer vacation period starting June and ending in September around Labor Day weekend. The neighborhood children having free time to enjoy doing anything imaginable could be possibility of total madness created from borderline insanity to boredom. This realization of creating something to do out of nothing began about a good 2 weeks into the scorching summer afternoon of July. This creation to exploit nature's heat wave found homeboys from Smith Street Projects hooking up to seek whatever possible good natural fun form of pleasure. This exciting thought less visionary event filled opportunity just so happened on a Tuesday.

This location surrounding the area turn out to be a generous size patch of dried grass formed because of drought like condition. This location was down the hill away from wooded area that was outstanding spot for a few bored homies searching for choosing recreational excitement for a little while during what seemed like an endless summer of boredom. A chosen plan agreed upon to get possible more bang for our bucks by all the homies became more popular as this blueprint continued to be expressed so vividly with such unimaginable thoughtless creativity presenting such an air of enormous excitement. This vivid portrayal focused on such energetic response captivating our total concentration in a flavorful spontaneous emotional display of happiness enhanced the ultimate feeling of being captured in a dream. The mindboggling experience expanded so thrillingly with immediate gratification glowing so beautifully upon the faces of these homies intense plan in a chaotic forgetfulness of summer heat baking our bodies. This spectacle shared unexpectedly for everyone suddenly started to create a loss of our composure from such a provoking source of energy being drained out of us suddenly left our mouth grasping for further words to express thrilling victory. The exhibit placed on display creating a startling vision of absolute surprise beyond recognition to visualize final method of increased joy and excitement finally removed from home boys front pocket came from a box of crackerjacks. This crackerjack box could be purchased at the corner store for a little chump change that might of amount to nickel or 5 cents. This chump change or nickel could be easily hustled by walking around the hood collecting empty glass bottles of (Pop) Pepsi, Coca Cola and Hires root beer soda. This awesome surprise item came in a caramel coated popcorn and sweet peanuts insured ultimate satisfaction with every sensation the bud in our mouth enjoying such a treat to increase popularity of crackerjack. Then finally seeing a reward laying at the bottom of a crackerjack box that helped to bring on more energetic appeal lasting far longer than this sweet sensation suddenly became a far reasoned revelation of a phenomenal to us home boys.

The location chosen to perform our summer ritual by homeboys happened to be an extraordinary place. This area was a short cut for traveling in the back of Smith Street projects instead of the front. This route helped us avoid the highway traffic going on in front area of Smith Street Project. This backyard paradise created so much excitement for adventure during the school year. We had choice to go one direction that lead to a creek running water which let us make a decision to cross over onto the other side. This crossing area had a wooden pole from one bank to another bank about 10 to 15 foot long. This pole lay above grass on top of dirt that would be capable of twisting while attempting to cross from one bank side to the other bank side with running creek water underneath the pole. Some homeboys would be standing on one side or the other side while a person tried crossing over on the pole to the other side. The homeboys being distracted while waiting their turn to cross over on this pole would begin throwing big rocks into rushing creek water. These big rocks would create splashing water onto pole creating slipping or falling into running creek water. These extracurricular activities happened while we should of have been heading to Warring School on Smith Street. The original path would have taken us on a dirt trail that had junkyard dogs always ready to run after us any season of the year.

This excitement continued while traveling in another direction leading us onto location chosen for our Summer ritual that had abandoned railroad cars on railroad tracks. We would go inside the abandon railroad cars searching for anything of value. This abandon railroad car had many gallon cans of fruit cocktail and peaches that had been left. We could carry these gifts home to enjoy the sweet delicious fruits until all these cans gone. The railroad tracks that no longer in operation lead us pass a lumber yard and salvage area for destroyed cars. Then while continuing onto school a little ways further on we saw more railroad tracks. This location had coal pockets which the running railroad cars came to unload coal. We became interested in more fun filled excitement by playing in these coal pockets before eventually making our last stop at a paper company across the street from coal yard. The journey to Warring School on Smith Street finally concluded for us to arrive on time to get on with our days learning in the class room.

The Summer Meltdown would actually happen as a result of the Crackerjack box containing a magnifying glass. The ritual actually began on a Tuesday afternoon on the dirt path that created so many eventful fun filled adventurous excitement. This Tuesday afternoon involved about four of us homeboys chilling underneath a shady tree. This tree would sometimes be an escape from the junkyard dogs running after us by jumping up to grab a branch for safety. We had been meeting many times on Tuesdays to enjoy this ritual that had never been discussed. Our homeboys house happened to be really close to this specific time for pulling out the magnifying glass. We knew results that happened from our previous fires that had been set on those hot summer afternoons with extremely dry grass. This sudden ignition from extremely dry grass thrilled everyone into watching so intensely that the decision to keep letting fire burn for spreading resulted in an uncontrollable event. We were absolutely amazed that this fire could not be put out by the four of us. We were lucky that no houses near by got burned down from our ritual that never again happened during this Summer Meltdown on Tuesdays.

Childhood picture going to Warring School in Poughkeepsie, New York.